Reading About
THE GRAY WOLF

Carol Greene

Content Consultant:
Dan Wharton, Ph.D., Curator,
New York Zoological Society

Reading Consultant:
Michael P. French, Ph.D.,
Bowling Green State University

ENSLOW PUBLISHERS, INC.

Bloy St. & Ramsey Ave.
Box 777
Hillside, N.J. 07205
U.S.A.

P.O. Box 38
Aldershot
Hants GU12 6BP
U.K.

Library of Congress Cataloging-in-Publication Data

Greene, Carol.
    Reading about the gray wolf / Carol Greene.
      p. cm. — (Friends in danger series)
    Includes index.
    Summary: Describes the gray wolf and its behavior, explains
its status as an endangered species, and suggests what can be done to
help save it.
    ISBN 0-89490-427-2
    1. Wolves—Juvenile literature. 2. Endangered species—Juvenile
literature. [1. Wolves. 2. Rare animals.] I. Title.
II. Series: Greene, Carol. Friends in danger series.
QL737.C22G73 1993
599.74'442—dc20   92-26800
                                            CIP
                                            AC

Printed in the United States of America

10 9 8 7 6 5 4 3 2 1

Photo Credits: ©The Bettmann Archive, p. 18; ©Michael Francis/The Wildlife Collection,
p. 10; D. Robert Franz/The Wildlife Collection, p. 16; ©Anne Fournier/Photo Researchers,
Inc., p. 8; ©Farrell Graham/Photo Researchers, Inc., p. 1; ©Eunice Harris/Photo Researchers, Inc., p. 20; ©Henry Holdsworth/The Wildlife Collection, Inc., p. 24; ©Thomas
Kitchin/Tom Stack & Associates, p. 12; ©Tom and Pat Leeson, pp. 22, 26; © Gary
Millburn/Tom Stack & Associates, p. 6; ©Brian Parker/Tom Stack & Associates, Inc., p.
4; ©Leonard Lee Rue III/Photo Researchers, Inc., p. 14.

Cover Photo Credit: ©Renee Lynn/Photo Researchers, Inc.

Photo Researcher: Grace How

CONTENTS

SMOKE

It is night.
The bright stars shine
and all is quiet.

Then, deep in the woods,
a large gray wolf
lifts his head and howls.

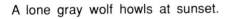
A lone gray wolf howls at sunset.

He is Smoke,
leader of the pack.
He is calling
the other wolves together.
It is time to hunt for food.

A pack is a family of wolves.
Most packs have seven
or eight wolves in them:
a father, a mother,
their young (called pups),
and some grown-up
sisters and brothers.
Packs are always changing
as young leave to find mates.

Wolves look a lot like dogs.

Pack members are loyal
to one another.
They hunt and play together.
Together they all feed
and care for the pups.

From close by, a wolf
howls back to Smoke.
Another howls from far away.
Wolves can hear howls
for several miles.

A wolf pack.

Smoke's mate howls too.
Her pups go "Yelp! Yelp!"
But they will not hunt.
The others will bring them food.

At last the pack is together.
They are not all gray.
The fur of gray wolves
can be white, black,
gray, rusty brown, or mixed.

A mother wolf and cub.

Smoke smells deer
and begins to run.
The others run with him.
Wolves can smell food
from over a mile away.
Their long legs run fast—
up to 50 miles an hour.

Smoke's pack finds four deer.
Three deer run away.
But one is sick.
She cannot run fast.
The wolves kill her quickly
with their sharp teeth.

A wolf pack sniffs for the smell of a deer.

They eat until they are full.
Then they bring food
back to the den.
The den is a little room
in the side of a hill.
A tunnel leads to it.

Smoke's pups tumble
out of the tunnel.
They are several weeks old.
Sometimes they still
drink their mother's milk.
But they need meat too.

A mother wolf can have
from four to fifteen pups.
Most have about six.
This is called a litter.

Two wolf pups peek out of their den.

Now everyone has eaten.
They all feel good.
Smoke begins to howl
and so do the others.
Why are they howling?
Just for fun.

A wolf howls.

DANGER!

For hundreds of years,
many people have
feared and hated wolves.
That is because they don't
know much about wolves.

These people are
wolves' worst enemies.

They shoot, trap,
and poison wolves.
They blow up dens
and kill the pups.

A wolf hunter carries his prize in the 1800s.

Native Americans called
wolves "brother" and "sister."
They knew wolves have
their own job in nature.

They knew that wolves
are good hunters.
Wolves kill sick
and weak animals.
This leaves the rest
of the herd stronger.

Native Americans respect gray wolves.
They know they are great hunters.

Once gray wolves lived
all over North America.
Now there are only
about 1,000 gray wolves
left in the United States,
except for Alaska.

About 5,000 gray wolves
live in Alaska and
about 7,000 in Canada.

Some people are trying
to put wolves back into
wild places in the U.S.
But others are fighting them.

Today, most gray wolves live in cold places
where there are not many people.

These people must learn
what Native Americans knew.
Wolves are important
to wild places.
They must give wolves
a chance to do
their job in nature.

A gray wolf sniffs a deer.

WHAT YOU CAN DO

1. Learn more about wolves. Read books and watch nature shows.

2. Visit a zoo or refuge. Sometimes you can see gray wolves there.

3. Some parks and refuges hold wolf howls in the fall. Leaders take people to the woods at night and let them listen to the wolves howling.

4. If you can't go to a howl, see if your library has a tape of wolves howling.

You can hear real wolves howl in some national parks.

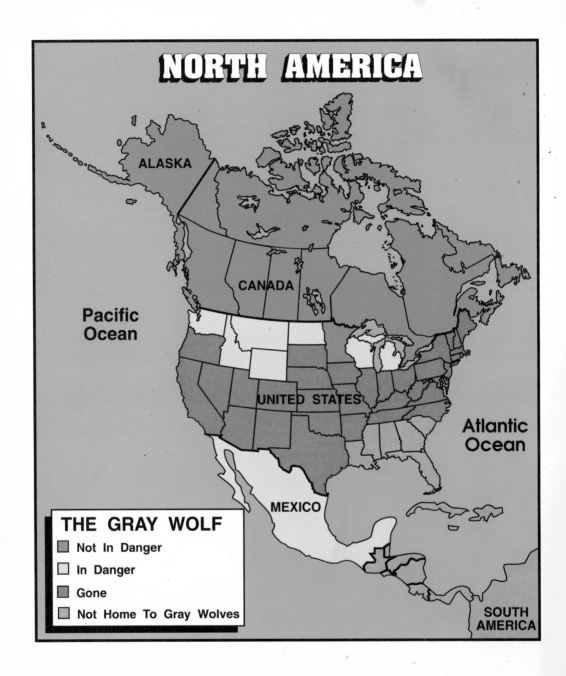

NORTH AMERICA

ALASKA

CANADA

Pacific
Ocean

UNITED STATES

Atlantic
Ocean

MEXICO

THE GRAY WOLF

Not In Danger

In Danger

Gone

Not Home To Gray Wolves

SOUTH
AMERICA

MORE FACTS ABOUT THE GRAY WOLF

- A female and male often stay together for life.

- Most gray wolves in the lower United States live in Minnesota. There are still a few in Michigan, Wisconsin, and Montana.

- Each pack has its own hunting area. The wolves like to eat big animals, such as moose and deer. But if they are very hungry, they will even eat mice.

- Pups learn to hunt when they are about 6 months old.

- Gray wolves are shy of people.

- Wolves may be the ancestors of dogs.

- An adult male gray wolf is 3 feet tall. He is almost 6-½ feet long. He weighs over 100 pounds. Females are a little smaller.

WORDS TO LEARN

ancestor—A relative who lived a long time ago.

den—A resting place for animals. For wolves it is a small room in the side of a hill.

gray wolf—A large, meat-eating member of the dog family. Its Latin name is *Canis lupus*.

herd—A group of wild animals, such as deer, that live together.

howl—A long, loud sound.

litter—A group of young wolves born at the same time.

pack—A family of wolves.

pup—A baby wolf.

refuge—A place where wild animals can live in safety.

INDEX